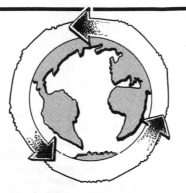

PROJECTS FOR A HEALTHY PLANET

Simple Environmental Experiments for Kids

Shar Levine

Allison Grafton

ILLUSTRATED BY TERRY CHUI

JOHN WILEY & SONS, INC.

New York   Chichester   Brisbane   Toronto   Singapore

In recognition of the importance of preserving what has been written, it is a policy of John Wiley & Sons, Inc., to have books of enduring value published in the United States printed on acid-free paper, and we exert our best efforts to that end.

6/93   J Fund 11⁰⁰

Copyright © 1992 by John Wiley & Sons, Inc.

This publication is designed to provide accurate and authoritative information in regard to the subject matter covered. It is sold with the understanding that the publisher is not engaged in rendering legal, accounting, or other professional service. If legal advice or other expert assistance is required, the services of a competent professional person should be sought. From a Declaration of Principles jointly adopted by a Committee of the American Bar Association and a Committee of Publishers.

Library of Congress Cataloging-in-Publication Data

Levine, Shar, 1953-
    Projects for a healthy planet: simple environmental experiments for kids/ Shar Levine, Allison Grafton; illustrated by Terry Chui.
        p.   cm.
    Includes index.
    Summary: Projects designed to help us understand causes of pollution, to protect our resources, and to create environmentally friendly products.
    ISBN 0-471-55484-7 (alk. paper)
    1. Environmental protection—Juvenile literature. 2. Environmental protection—Experiments—Juvenile literature. [1. Environmental protection—Experiments. 2. Experiments.] I. Grafton, Allison. II. Chui, Terry, ill. III. Title.
TD171.7.L48 1992
628'.078—dc20   91-42406

Printed in the United States of America

10 9 8 7 6 5 4 3

The Publisher and the author have made every reasonable effort to ensure that the experiments and activities in this book are safe when conducted as instructed but assume no responsibility for any damage caused or sustained while performing the experiments or activities in *Projects for a Healthy Planet*. Parents, guardians, and/or teachers should supervise young readers who undertake the experiments and activities in this book.

This book is dedicated to my husband Paul, and my children Shira and Joshua for their love, support, and inspiration and to my parents, Dorothy and Max Levine, for their belief and encouragement. My thanks to Allison and Terry, two exceptional and gifted people.

Shar Levine

This book is dedicated to my parents, Nicky and George Grafton, for their love, support, and belief in me, to my entire family, and to Kevin Taillefer for his love and understanding.

My thanks to Shar and Terry for their creativity, energy, and cooperation. Without them this book would not have been possible.

Allison Grafton

I dedicate this book to my parents, On and Kuk Ho Chui, and my entire family for their support and encouragement. A special thanks to Shar Levine and her family for their belief in me, and their help while providing a home for wayward artists.

I'd also like to thank Allison, Sarah, Paula, and Andrea for putting up with me at Einstein's and critiquing my work.

Many thanks to Herb, Nancy, Lisa, and Bonni for keeping me on my toes at Cap.

Thank you one and all.

Terry Chui

ACKNOWLEDGMENTS

The authors would also like to thank Paula Smisko, who held down the fort while we wrote this book, Allan MacDougall and his staff, Maurice Bridge and Ellen Rosenberg for their help, Sarah Hamblin for her advice, George Atamian for his energy, and Harold Urist and the law firm of Rosenberg Rosenberg.

A special thanks to the many children who have taken classes at Einstein's the Science Centre and who have been instrumental in testing the experiments.

And to Paul Lambert—hello Lambert!

CONTENTS

INTRODUCTION

Look outside. What you see is your environment—the soil, the trees, the water, the buildings, even the sky. Everything you do affects it, from turning on a light to riding in an automobile.

Some of the effects can easily be seen, like smoke in the air. Others occur farther away, where rain falls on the forests and where rivers are dammed for hydroelectric energy.

And with so many of us living together, all those effects together can make a major difference to our environment. In parts of the country, the environmental balance has been upset.

The simple fact is that we have to look after our environment, and we all have to do this in our own way. There are ways to solve environmental problems, not the least of which is to avoid making matters worse.

This book is designed to help you understand some of the causes of pollution and examine alternatives to the use of nonrenewable resources, and to help you create environmentally friendly products.

In the process, you'll learn a lot about the science involved in the natural world, and in the products we manufacture.

You'll also have a lot of fun doing the experiments.

A note on the step-by-step drawings: At the beginning of each experiment are drawings of the materials needed. Common household things used in the experiments, like paper and pencils, are not illustrated.

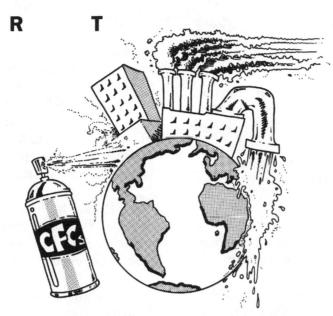

SOMETHING'S HAPPENING HERE
Pollution and the Environment

So that you can fully understand and appreciate the experiments and activities you're going to be doing, you should remember this: YOU make a difference.

Pollution is caused by many people—one at a time—forgetting to care for the environment. The solution works the same way: people—one at a time—can stop pollution and help the environment. And by learning how the environment works, we can help others learn and act.

Here are some ways to stop the biggest pollution problems.

ACID RAIN

Acid rain is rain that catches pollutants in the atmosphere and carries them back to Earth where they poison our waters, destroy trees, eat away at buildings and statues, harm our soil, and kill fish and plants. Here's how you can help cut down on the amount of acid rain created.

1 Use less fuel—walk, take a bus, ride a bike, or carpool. The less pollution you put into the air, the less acid rain there will be.

2 Waste less. Turn down your thermostat in the winter as far as you can without feeling uncomfortable and try not to use an air conditioner in the summer. Recycle, and don't buy products that are overpackaged or whose packaging can't be recycled.

OZONE DEPLETION

The ozone layer is a layer of gas located high above the Earth that protects us from the harmful rays of the sun. Ozone is being destroyed faster than it is being created. Now there is a hole in the ozone layer that cannot be repaired. There are things that you can do to help prevent the hole from getting any larger.

1 Ask your parents to keep any cooling appliances in good repair. The cooling systems in freezers, air conditioners, and refrigerators contain chemicals called CFCs (chlorofluorocarbons) that can escape and eat up the ozone layer.

2 Do not buy products that contain any polystyrene. These include such things as foam fast-food containers and egg cartons.

3 Although CFCs in aerosol cans have been banned, many aerosol products still contain them; read the labels and avoid these products.

SMOG

Smog is air polluted by the fumes given off by cars, factories, and other things that burn fuel. Smog can make people sick, and it encourages the *greenhouse effect*—hot air gets trapped near the Earth, and the planet's atmosphere gets hotter and hotter. The greenhouse effect is causing temperatures around the world to increase. There are things you can do to help.

1 If you have to use a car to get somewhere, make sure that your parents keep it in good repair. But better yet, don't use a car. Walk, bike, carpool, or take the train.

2 Do not barbecue with charcoal; use a gas grill.

3 Mow your lawn with a mower that uses human power, rather than gas or electricity. It's cheaper, quieter, and causes no pollution.

4 Plant a tree! Trees clean our air and make oxygen for us to breathe.

GARBAGE

Garbage control is probably the easiest way to get involved in cleaning up the environment. There are so many ways to help.

1 Don't buy as much. Live by the saying "Make it do; use it up; wear it out." Then you won't waste as much.

2 Buy environmentally friendly products—ones that aren't overpackaged and don't cause any harm to the environment when they are used. You can also make your own environmentally friendly products by using experiments in this book!

3 Buy products that come in packaging (including bottles) that can be reused or recycled.

4 Buy paper products instead of plastic ones. Try to buy recycled-paper products.

5 Compost your food wastes. (See the Earth(worm) Day experiment.) You will make a rich fertilizer for your garden and create less garbage for landfills.

6 Get involved in your community's recycling program. If your community doesn't have one, organize one, or write to your city government and ask for one. You could also start a recycling program in your school, and ask your parents to start one in their offices.

7 Take your lunch to school or camp in reusable containers, including drink canteens and sandwich boxes.

8 Cut up plastic six-pack rings before you throw them in the garbage; try to recycle them. Better yet, don't buy cans of soft drinks that are held in plastic rings. Animals can get trapped in them and hurt themselves.

9 Take your own cloth or string bags when you go shopping, or reuse the plastic or paper bags you got the last time you went to the store.

WATER POLLUTION

By polluting our lakes, rivers, and oceans, we are poisoning our water supply. The water cycle helps to clean itself, but there is only so much pollution that our waters can take. Here's how you can help clean up our water supply.

1 Don't dump harmful liquids or chemicals onto the ground or into the sink or toilet. This includes disinfectants, cleaners, paints, motor oils, or other things that contain chemicals. Contact your local sanitation department for instructions on how to get rid of these things safely.

2 Conserve water whenever possible:

—Don't let the water run when you're brushing your teeth.

—Take a short shower instead of a bath.

—Wash the car with a sponge and a pail of water instead of water running from a hose.

—Don't overwater lawns, and water only during the mornings or evenings to avoid evaporation.

—Don't ask for a glass of water in a restaurant if you aren't going to drink it.

—Collect rainwater for gardens.

3 Don't use phosphate detergents.

ENERGY

There are different types of energy that we can use. Some energy is from renewable sources and does not harm the environment when used; some energy is nonrenewable and can be harmful to the environment when used (see *Smog* and *Ozone* sections). Here are some ways that you can conserve energy.

1 Always put a full load of wash in the washer, not a small load. Use cold water to wash your clothes whenever possible.

2 Dry clothes on a line instead of in the dryer, when weather permits.

3 Ask your parents to have your house and windows insulated well. This cuts down on the energy needed to heat your home.

4 Turn off lights, televisions, radios, and other electrical appliances when you're not using them.

SCHOOL OR GROUP ACTIVITIES

1 Plan Earth Day events at your school or in your community.

2 Have a special science fair just for environmental projects.

3 Have a contest in your community for environmental posters, stories, and helpful ideas. Get businesses to donate prizes.

4 Have your school or class adopt a polluted area and organize a cleanup.

5 Organize a "watchdog committee" from your class to report on pollution in your school or community.

6 Start a class project. Have your class write letters to the government asking for tougher laws against polluters.

7 Join an environmental group and get involved. Bring along a friend—the Earth needs all the help it can get!

Now that you know what you can do to help stop pollution, happy experimenting!

13

ACID RAIN

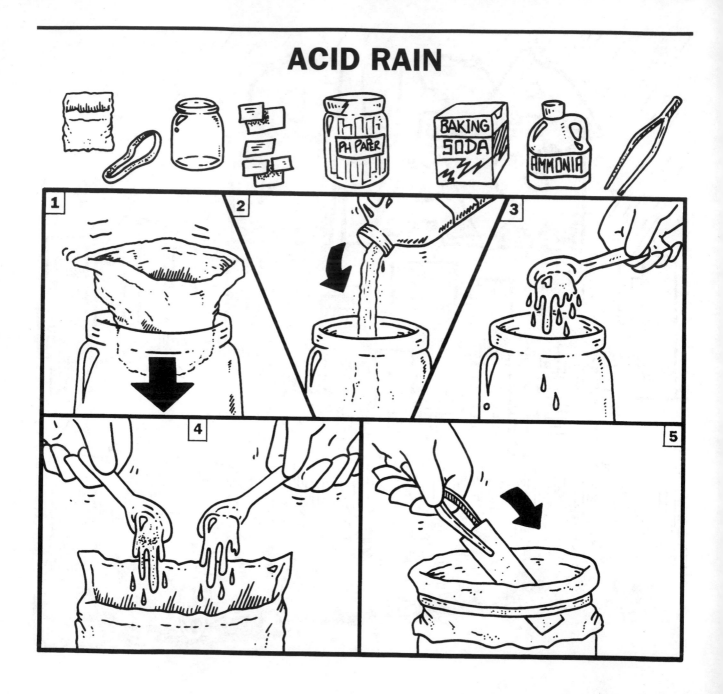

Everyone can see smog or smell polluted air, but not everyone knows if acid rain is affecting their area. You can't see it and you can't smell it, but acid rain causes great damage to the Earth. Sulphur dioxide from coal-burning industrial plants and nitrogen oxides from car exhausts rise up through the air and create clouds. These clouds can then be blown anywhere the wind goes. Along the way, these clouds mix with water vapor, heat from the sun, and oxygen to change into substances that are highly acidic. The water vapor in these acid-laden clouds can fall to Earth as rain, snow, sleet, or any other type of precipitation. Here's a simple way to see if the rain, snow, or waters near your home are acidic.

Materials

2 plastic sandwich bags

10 small glass jars or drinking glasses

rubber band

10 small squares of paper to make labels

tape

a freshly collected sample of either rain; lake, river, or pond water; or melted snow

small amounts of the following (about 1 tablespoon [15 ml] of each): lemon juice; apple juice; cola; coffee; milk; cooled, boiled water; baking soda; milk of magnesia; ammonia

red cabbage indicator (recipe follows) or pH paper (litmus paper)

tweezers

What to do

1 Put a plastic sandwich bag inside a small glass jar, being very careful not to touch the inside of the bag. Put a rubber band around the edge of the jar to hold the bag in place. Then collect the sample as follows: Rain: Place the jar outside in the rain. Make sure it is in a clear, open space, away from any trees, buildings, or power poles. Snow: Either place the jar outside in an open space while it is snowing, or scoop a sample of freshly fallen snow into your container. Lake, river, or pond water: With an adult's assistance, take a sample of water several feet from the bank and several inches below the surface. On a piece of paper, write the kind of water, and record the date and time of collection. Use cellophane tape to attach the label to the jar.

2.0	3.0	4.0	5.0	6.0	7.0	8.5	10.0	12.0
lemon juice	apple juice	cola	coffee	milk	boiled water	baking soda	milk of magnesia	ammonia

Low pH   ←   More Acid   More Alkaline   →   High pH

2 Label 9 jars, in order, and fill with small amounts of the following household liquids (from low to high pH): lemon juice (pH 2.0); apple juice (pH 3.0); cola (pH 4.0); coffee (pH 5.0); milk (pH 6.0); cooled, boiled water (pH 7.0); baking soda (pH 8.5); milk of magnesia (pH 10.0); and ammonia (pH 12.0). The lower the pH, the more *acidic* a substance is. The higher the pH, the more *alkaline,* or *basic,* a substance is. A pH of 7.0 means that a substance is *neutral.*

3 Add 1 tablespoon (15 ml) of red cabbage juice to each jar. You should see a range of colors from the different samples.

4 Place 1 tablespoon (15 ml) of red cabbage juice in a clean plastic sandwich bag. Add 1 tablespoon (15 ml) of your water sample to it. Compare the color of this sample to those of the household liquids. The one that comes closest to the color of the water sample will tell you how acidic it is.

5 You may also use pH paper to test how acidic your sample is. You can buy strips of pH paper from hobby shops or drugstores. To test your sample, hold one end of the pH paper with a pair of tweezers, and place the other end of the strip into your freshly collected water sample. Allow some time for the pH paper to change colors. Compare the changed color of the pH paper to the color chart on the pH paper container. A pH of 5.0 to 5.6 means that the water sample that you collected is unpolluted by acid rain.

What happened

Red cabbage juice and pH papers are called *indicators*. An *indicator* tells you whether something is an acid or a base. If the red cabbage juice turns pink, the thing that you are testing is an acid; if it turns blue, it is a base. The sample you are testing is called neutral if there is no color change. If your water is unpolluted by acid rain, it will match the pH paper or red cabbage indicator for the milk or coffee. If it is polluted by acid rain, it will match the apple juice or lemon juice.

How to make red cabbage indicator

You'll need an adult to help you with this.

Materials

red cabbage (about 2 cups)   strainer
saucepan   large jar

Finely slice or grate about 2 cups (480 ml) of red cabbage; place in a saucepan, and cover with about 2 cups (480 ml) of water. Put this on the stove and bring to a boil. Turn off the heat, and let the mixture cool. When cool, strain the liquid into the jar and throw out the cabbage. The red cabbage juice can now be used for your experiment.

THE SOILING OF ACID RAIN

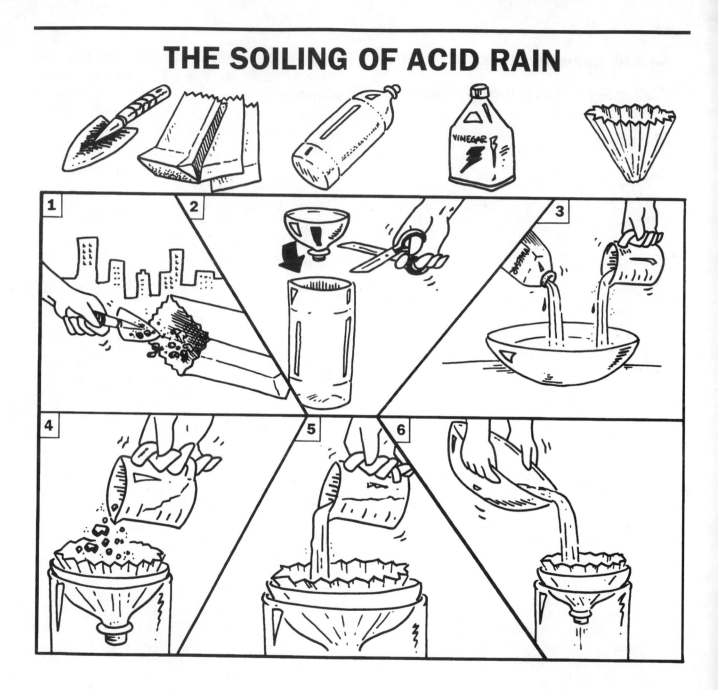

Soils can naturally neutralize—cut down the acidity of—rain. But the soil's ability to neutralize does not last forever. Let's see what effect acid rain has already had on the soil around your home.

Materials

scoop or trowel
soil samples
small paper bags
2-liter plastic soda bottle
vinegar
neutral water (cooled, boiled water)
bowl
pH papers or red cabbage indicator (see Acid Rain experiment)
coffee filters

What to do

1 Use a scoop or trowel to collect about 2 cups (480 ml) of soil from different areas around your city or home. Put each sample in a paper bag, and label the bag indicating the place you took it from. If you wish, you may also use store-bought potting soil as one of your samples.

2 Have an adult cut the top 4 inches (10 cm) off the 2-liter plastic bottle, and fit it upside down into the rest of the bottle to form a funnel.

3 Make a solution of 1 cup (240 ml) each of water and vinegar in a bowl. Measure the pH value. You want the mixture to have a pH value of 4. If the pH is not 4, add more water or vinegar and check again. This is your imitation acid rain solution.

4 Put a coffee filter in the funnel, and fill it with about 1 cup (240 ml) of soil.

5 Pour some neutral water through the funnel until about ¹/₂ cup (120 ml) has filtered through the soil. Remove the funnel. Measure the pH of the water and record it.

6 Rinse the bottle and replace the funnel. Pour some of the acid rain solution over the soil, and let it drip through the funnel until approximately ¹/₂ cup (120 ml) of liquid has dripped through. Measure the pH value of the liquid, and record it. Rinse the bottle out and perform the experiment again with a different soil sample.

What happened

Some soils have a greater ability than others to neutralize the acidity of the rain. Other soils may have already been so affected by pollution that they have lost their ability to buffer the acidity of the mixture. Some soils may naturally be more acidic, depending on where the sample was taken from.

Did you know?

Acid rain has been recorded with the same pH as battery acid, and there has even been fog with the same pH as lemon juice. Acid rain has caused some lakes to have the same pH value as cola. Do you think that your goldfish could survive in cola?

To solve the acid rain problem, we need fewer emissions from car engines and from factories. Each time you walk or ride a bike to go somewhere, you're helping to keep the environment clean.

Some of the damage that acid rain has caused to lakes, rivers, and streams can be fixed. If acid rain stops flowing into the affected waters and the damage to the waterways isn't too great, then life can come back to these areas.

OZONE: HERE COMES THE SUN

There are different kinds of ozone. The ozone floating in the stratosphere is a "good" kind of ozone, while the ozone that comes out the back of cars is not good. The ozone layer surrounding the Earth protects us from the harmful rays of the sun (the ones that give us a sunburn). This ozone layer is being destroyed by chemicals called chlorofluorocarbons (CFCs) that have been released into the air. As this ozone layer thins, more people are being hurt by the sun's rays. This experiment will help illustrate the need to protect your skin from the damaging rays of the sun.

Materials

scraps of window-tinting film of different
    strengths or different tints of cellophane
large piece of black cardboard or poster board
scissors
masking tape
clear plastic wrap
newspaper

What to do

1 Collect several different scraps of window-tinting film, each of different tinting strengths. Most auto-glass or home-glass tinting companies are happy to give you these scraps. You do not need the glass, only the plastic film from the top of the glass.

2 Cut holes in the black cardboard, slightly smaller than each of the scraps you have collected, and tape the scraps to the cardboard.

3 Cut another hole in the cardboard, and cover this hole with clear plastic wrap.

4 Place the cardboard with the tinted windows over a new piece of newspaper. Place the cardboard-covered newspaper in the sun.

5 At the end of one day's exposure, carefully lift the cardboard from the paper, and observe the way that the newspaper has faded under each of the windows.

6 Put the experiment back together, as it was before, and place it out in the sun for another day. What differences are there after two days?

What happened

Newsprint is sensitive to the sun's rays and will change color (or turn yellow) when exposed to the sun. The different tinted films blocked out the sun's rays and prevented the newspaper from yellowing. Sunscreens protect people's skin in the same way. The sun's harmful rays are blocked from our skin, and the safe rays are allowed in.

GOING, GOING, GONE: OZONE 2

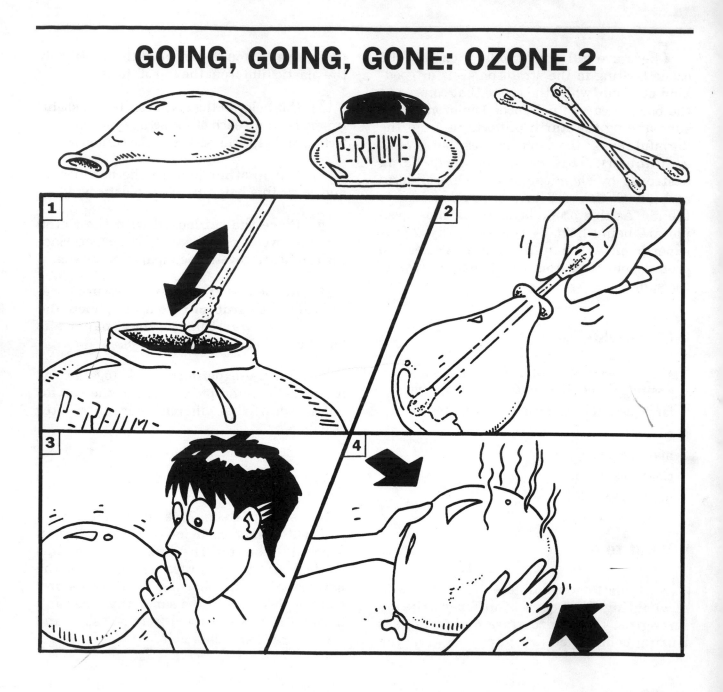

How do the CFCs float up so high that they begin to destroy the ozone layer? To give you an idea of how chemicals can travel through the air, try this experiment.

Materials

balloon
perfume
cotton swab

What to do

1 Find the open end of the balloon. Ask permission to borrow some perfume and dip one end of the cotton swab into the perfume.

2 Insert the same end of the swab into the opening of the balloon. Smear the swab around inside the balloon. Do not do this too close to the mouth of the balloon, or the perfume will get into your mouth when you blow up the balloon.

3 Blow up the balloon, and tie the neck of the balloon tightly.

4 Gently squeeze the balloon between your hands. What do you smell?

What happened

The molecules in the perfume were so tiny that they escaped through the membrane of the balloon. This shows how gases can escape from sealed containers and rise into the air to reach the ozone layer. Even if the world stopped using CFCs today, the destruction of the ozone layer would continue for years. It takes 25 years for the CFCs to rise into the atmosphere and 100 years for them to disappear. A Scary Fact: One man was partially responsible for creating the world's greatest environmental problems. A chemist named Thomas Midgley not only recommended replacing poisonous ammonia in refrigerators with CFCs, but he also proposed adding lead to gasoline. These two applications led to the breakdown in the ozone layer, increased air pollution, and the greenhouse effect.

Did you know?

Elephants are smarter than people (when it comes to protecting themselves from the sun). Elephants have sensitive skin and they protect their skin from the harmful rays of the sun by covering their bodies with mud. This acts as a natural sunscreen. So be smart like the elephant, and protect yourself from the sun by wearing a hat and sunscreen.

THE UNDETECTABLES

Every day, sewage, chemicals, and other wastes are being pumped into the world's water supply. This water pollution is affecting not only fish but all life on Earth—and it's not always easy to detect. Here's one way to see how polluted water can get into food.

Materials

fresh celery with leaves
knife
2 glasses of clear apple juice
red and blue food coloring

What to do

1 Have an adult cut off the bottom from a piece of celery. Then divide the celery in half lengthwise, leaving about 2 inches (5 cm) below the leaves not split.

2 Fill the 2 glasses halfway with apple juice. Add 3 drops of red food coloring to one, and 3 drops of blue food coloring to the other.

3 Gently place one-half of the celery in each glass, and let stand for several hours.

4 Take the celery out and carefully cut the celery into slices. You'll be able to see how far the "polluted" water traveled up the celery stalk. Near the top of the stalk, you'll see that there are two colors in the veins.

5 Taste the celery. Can you taste the apple juice?

Try this experiment again. But this time use water and food coloring instead of the apple juice.

What happened

Plants take water from the soil through their roots and stems. This water contains moisture and minerals that a plant needs to grow. If the water is polluted, the plant could also absorb the pollution. Any living things—birds, fish, animals, or people—that eat plants that have a polluted water source are also taking in these pollutants. Even though the celery soaked up the apple juice, you could not taste it. And you can't taste if any pollutants made their way into your food either.

Did you know?

When you look at a photograph of the Earth taken from space, it looks as if most of the Earth's surface is covered with water. It is—70 percent of the Earth's surface is water. But, of this water, 97 percent is salt water, 3 percent is fresh water, and only 1 percent is available for drinking water. Rain washes pollutants such as pesticides, artificial fertilizers, chemicals from industry, and toxic wastes into rivers, lakes, and oceans, where they can contaminate the water supply. Any living thing that gets water from a polluted source is also affected. It only takes a tiny amount of pollutants to make a huge amount of water unsafe to drink.

A FRIENDLY OIL SPILL

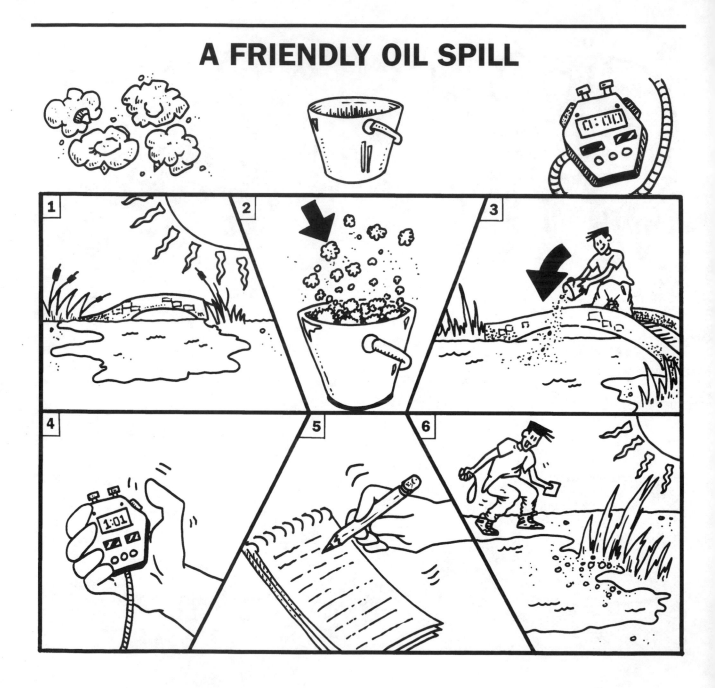

The short-term effects of an oil spill are easy to see. The black tarlike oil washes up on beaches. It covers the sand, rocks, and plants. Birds, marine animals, and plants die when covered with this oil. Animals that eat the oil-coated plants, fish, or birds also become contaminated or poisoned. No matter how big or how small they are, oil spills are bad news for the environment. To see how much of the environment can be affected, here's a friendly way to create your own "oil spill" without causing any harm to the environment.

Materials

stale, unbuttered, unsalted popcorn

small plastic pail

stopwatch or watch with a second hand

What to do

Because this experiment will be performed near water, have an adult supervise you.

1 Find a small pond or lake where you can perform this experiment.

2 Fill the pail with popcorn.

3 Find a safe place to stand on the shore, or stand on a bridge if there is one available. Throw the popcorn into the water.

4 Time the popcorn to see how long it takes to spread out.

5 Take notes about what the popcorn becomes attached to.

6 If possible, follow the spill to see where it goes and what it touches.

What happened

Throwing popcorn into water is a safe way to show the impact of oil spills on the environment. (The popcorn will easily decompose and not pollute the water.) Imagine that the popcorn is really oil. Did you see how fast the "slick" spread through the water and how many plants, rocks, and objects it touched? What effect do you think that a real oil spill might have had on the plants, fish, and animals that live in and on the water? In an oil spill, wave action causes oil to coat plants, shorelines, birds, animals, and anything else that the oil touches.

Did you know?

On average, less than 10 percent of the oil in any spill can be cleaned up. If you think that's bad, just consider this: The amount of oil dumped into the ground every three weeks by people changing their own car oil is about 11 million gallons (about 41,000 kl). This is equal to the amount of oil spilled by the Exxon *Valdez* (a huge oil tanker that spilled oil in Alaska).

BREAKDOWN

Some stores advertise that their plastic bags are *biodegradable*. That means that when the bags are thrown away and put into landfills, they will begin to break down. How true is this?

Materials

1 cup (240 ml) milk

small saucepan

$1/4$ cup (60 ml) white vinegar

biodegradable plastic bag

nonbiodegradable plastic bag

paper and pen

sticks

tape

plastic wrap

small space in a garden

scoop or garden trowel

What to do

1 Have an adult help you warm the milk slightly in the saucepan over low heat until small bubbles appear at the edge. Do not boil! Remove from the heat. Slowly pour the vinegar into the milk and let sit. It will separate into a clear liquid and a white blob. Use a spoon to gently collect the white blob into one area. Carefully remove it from the pot and shape it into a ball. Allow this "milk plastic" to harden.

2 Get one regular plastic bag and one biodegradable plastic bag.

3 Label 3 pieces of paper as follows: "milk plastic," "biodegradable plastic," and "nonbiodegradable plastic." Tape each of these labels to a stick and cover with plastic wrap to protect against rain.

4 With an adult's permission, dig 3 holes about 5 inches (12.5 cm) deep in the garden. Add a little water to each hole.

5 Bury a piece of plastic about the same size in each of the holes. Place the correct marker by each hole. Fill the holes with soil.

6 If possible, you should water your experiment every two days or so.

7 After a month, dig up the plastics and see which ones have started to break apart. If you don't see any major changes, rebury them and check on them in another week.

What happened

The milk plastic that you made broke down long before the other two plastics. This is because of the chemical makeup of the plastic. While the biodegradable plastic may break down next, it still may be harming the environment because the inks used for the printing, as well as the chemical used to dry the inks, may be poisonous.

Did you know?

The first plastics were made from milk and plants. They weren't very strong, so newer, stronger plastics were developed. These plastics are made from oil and do not break down. Many people are trying to recycle plastics, which is a good thing, but it won't solve the problem completely. This is because each time a plastic is recycled, it can't be used to remake the same product. It has to be used to make a limited number of objects like benches, fence posts, or paint brushes.

No matter how many plastics we recycle, we still have to create new plastics to replace the old products, and that uses up oil. The best thing that we can do is to cut down our use of disposable plastic products and to use things like paper or cloth bags, cardboard boxes, and cloth diapers instead. Plastic kills over a million birds and tens of thousands of marine mammals yearly because it is mistaken by the animal for food.

WHAT'S EATING YOU?

Many great monuments, statues, and famous buildings all over the world are being destroyed by polluted air. It is sad to see beautiful carvings, made thousands of years ago, being eaten away by chemicals. Here's an experiment to help you understand some of the conditions that cause statues to erode.

Materials

3 pennies and 1 dime

fine sandpaper (or nail file)

3 paper clips

pencil

paper towel

small glass bowl

salt (about 1 tsp)

vinegar

plastic wrap

masking tape

What to do

1 Using sandpaper, rub all the surfaces of the pennies to make them clean. Straighten three paper clips and clean them also with the sandpaper.

2 Wrap one of the straightened paper clips around a pencil so that it forms a coil. Slide the coil off the pencil and save it. Wrap one clip around a penny and the last clip around the dime.

3 Fold a paper towel into quarters, and place it in the bottom of the glass bowl.

4 Place the penny with the paper clip wrapped around it, the coil, the two other plain pennies, and the dime on the towel.

5 Sprinkle the towel with water until it is completely wet. Then sprinkle the salt on the wet towel and add enough vinegar to totally cover the pennies, the dime, and the coil.

6 Tightly cover the bowl with the plastic wrap and seal the wrap to the bowl with masking tape. Watch the experiment over the next few days and keep track of the changes that you see occurring.

What happened

You have created an environment in the bowl that is similar to that found around the Statue of Liberty or any other monument located near an ocean. The plastic wrap seals in the moisture. The vinegar's effect is the same as the pollution in the air from industry. The salty water is like the ocean's spray. Many statues are made from copper and iron. The chemicals in the pollution combined with the salty water erode the copper and iron.

Did you know?

All over the world, monuments made of bronze, limestone, marble, and sandstone are being eaten away by pollution. Monuments such as Mount Rushmore, the Statue of Liberty, the Great Wall of China, and the Egyptian pyramids are being destroyed. Many monuments turn black or corrode when subjected to pollution. The face of the Sphinx in Egypt is rapidly being destroyed.

Monuments that have lasted through wars, weather, and natural disasters are being lost. If pollution is doing this to statues, just think what it is doing to the environment and to us!

WASTE NOT, WANT NOT
Conserve, Reuse, Recycle

To give you an idea of how much garbage each person throws away in a year, for one week try this simple experiment by yourself or with your family. If it's too difficult for one week, try it for one day!

Start on Monday morning. Whatever you would normally toss in the garbage, place in a large biodegradable trash bag instead. Take a trash bag with you wherever you go for this week. Label 9 more bags as listed on the next page. Each night, sort the garbage in your trash bag, and place the garbage in the proper labeled bag. Keep the bags in a cool place and closed with a bag tie.

1 *Organic*—vegetables, fruits, coffee grounds, tea bags, and eggshells

2 *Biodegradable*—meat, bones, milk products, fish, leftover foods, breads, pastas, and any other food wastes (other than the organic food wastes listed in **1**)

3 *Paper*—newspapers, any magazines or flyers, cardboard (including egg cartons), tissues, mail, milk cartons, cereal boxes, and so on

4 *Plastics*—foam containers (such as fast-food containers and meat trays), all plastic containers (such as milk jugs and soda bottles), empty rigid containers (like shampoo bottles), plastic shopping bags, broken plastic toys, and so on

5 *Garden*—grass, leaves, branches, and garden wastes

6 *Metal*—tin cans, aluminum cans, old pots

7 *Glass*—glass jars, bottles, or other containers (not light bulbs, mirrors, or dishes)

8 *Clothes*—old clothes and rags (Give usable old clothes to charity.)

9 *Mystery bag*—items that don't seem to belong in any other bag

If you fill up a labeled bag, start a second one for that category.

At the end of the week, weigh each bag and record the weights. Which bag weighs the most? Which the least? Total the weight of the bags. If you're anything like the average American, the total weight of your bags is probably about 28 pounds (12.7 kg) for the week. You probably created about 4 pounds (1.8 kg) of garbage each day. If you did this with your whole family, divide the total weight by the number of people in the family. The average should be about 28 pounds (12.7 kg) per person.

Now, total the weight of the bags containing the organic, paper, glass, metal, clothes, and garden wastes. Materials in these bags are reusable and do not need to be dumped in landfills. Food wastes are biodegradable, but aren't good for compost heaps. How heavy is the bag with the plastics? This should be your smallest bag if you are careful about your shopping. Who created the most garbage in your family? Why do you think that is? Now that you understand how sorting works, won't it be easy to start a recycling program in your home and school?

HOW GREEN IS MY GREENHOUSE?

The climate inside a greenhouse is warm, moist, and comfortable. Not only do plants grow faster in a greenhouse, but you can grow more plants and use less water and less energy than if you grew them outdoors. You also use fewer chemicals and pesticides, since the greenhouse provides a safer environment and gives the plants a warm and happy home in which to grow. Let's examine the difference between the temperature in a greenhouse and the outside temperature.

Materials

long strip of thick cardboard
stapler
large bowl, about 6 inches (15 cm) deep,
    with a rounded bottom
small pebbles or gravel
charcoal briquettes—crushed
soil
6 seedlings or small plants
2 thermometers
2 small sticks
plastic wrap
masking tape

What to do

1 Make a base for the bowl by cutting a 2-inch-wide (5 cm) strip of heavy cardboard that is long enough so that when it is stapled into a circle and the bowl is rested on it, the bowl will sit 1 inch (2.5 cm) off the table. Staple the ends of the strip so that it forms a circle. Place the bowl on the base. (NOTE: The cardboard must be sturdy enough to support the weight of the bowl and its contents.)

2 Line the bottom of the bowl with a layer of pebbles or gravel that is about 1 inch (2.5 cm) deep.

3 Next add about $1/2$ inch (1.25 cm) of crushed charcoal briquettes and 2 inches (5 cm) of soil to the bowl.

4 Bury seedlings or small plants 1 inch (2.5 cm) into the soil.

5 Lightly water the soil. Tape a small thermometer to a small stick and push the stick into the soil. (Do not bury any of the thermometer.) Mount another thermometer somewhere out of the sun but near the greenhouse.

6 Tightly seal the bowl, using plastic wrap and taping the edges so that no air can escape. Tilt the bowl slightly toward the sun. Keep a diary of the temperature inside and outside the greenhouse. Check the temperature several times during the day and one hour after the sun has gone down. If your seal is not tight, you may have to add a little water to the greenhouse. When your seedlings are about 2 inches (5 cm) high, you can transplant them to a larger container or put them into the garden (if there is no danger of frost).

What happened

Heat from the sun warmed the air inside the greenhouse during the day. This warm, moist air was trapped inside the greenhouse by the plastic wrap, making the air inside the greenhouse hotter than the air outside. This is one of the reasons that plants grow faster inside a greenhouse.

Did you know?

While a greenhouse environment is good for plants, the greenhouse effect is terrible for the Earth's environment. The burning of coal, oil, and other fuels produces carbon dioxide and other forms of pollution. These gases and particles form a layer of pollution that traps the sun's heat inside the Earth's atmosphere. The Earth's temperature is rising, and this changes the weather and climates all over the world. Planting trees helps slow down the greenhouse effect and reduces the carbon dioxide pollution. A tree can absorb as much as 50 pounds (23 kg) of carbon dioxide each year.

WINDPOWER

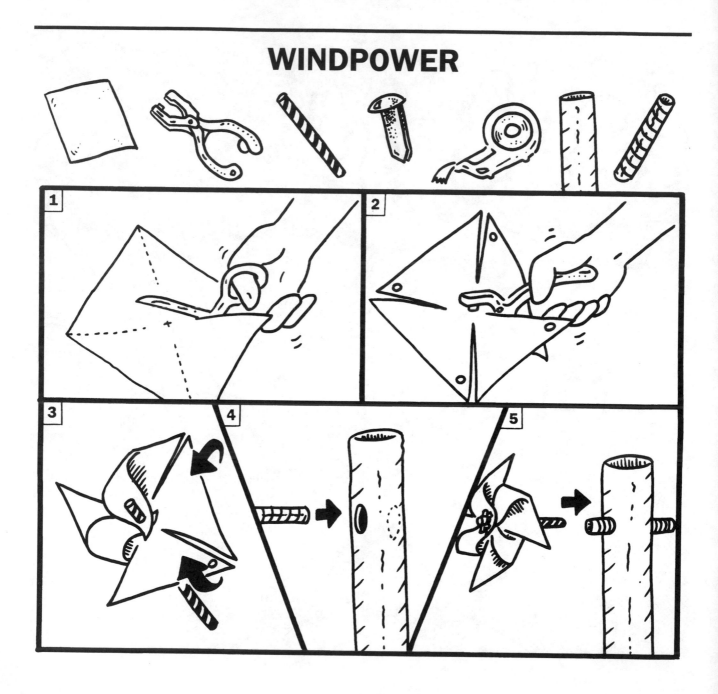

50

The first wind-powered machines were built around 600 B.C. Windmills were first used for grinding corn around A.D. 600, and windmills were later used throughout Europe in farming and in industry. Today, many states are using wind-powered turbines. Windmills are an environmentally safe and pollution-free source of energy.

Did you ever think that a simple pinwheel could perform work? In this activity, you will make a pinwheel. Then in the next one, you'll see what it can do.

Materials

construction paper

scissors

hole punch

small straw

brass paper fastener (available at stationery stores)

cardboard paper-towel roll

cellophane tape

large straw (big enough to fit the smaller straw inside)

What to do

1 Cut a piece of construction paper 6 inches (15 cm) square. Carefully fold it diagonally from top left to bottom right, and from bottom left to top right, then cut along the fold lines, stopping about 1 inch (2.5 cm) from the center of the square.

2 Punch a hole about ½ inch (1.25 cm) in from the corner of the right-hand side of each triangle. Gently slide the hole punch between the cut edges of two of the triangles and punch a hole in the center of the paper square.

3 Push the small straw through the center hole. Carefully bend each triangle, and push the hole over the straw. When all four holes have been pushed over the straw, slide the bent paper fastener into the end of the straw and tape the blunt end to the pinwheel. The pinwheel and straw should now turn together.

4 Measure down about 2 inches (5 cm) from the end of the paper-towel roll and punch two holes (large enough for the large straw to fit through) directly across from each other. Cut the larger straw so that it is about 4 inches (10 cm) long. Slide the larger straw through the openings in the paper-towel roll.

5 Slide the smaller straw (with the pinwheel on the end) into the larger straw and spin it several times to make sure it turns easily. If your pinwheel doesn't spin freely, adjust the hole openings slightly. Then try it again.

WEIGHT LIFTING WITH WIND

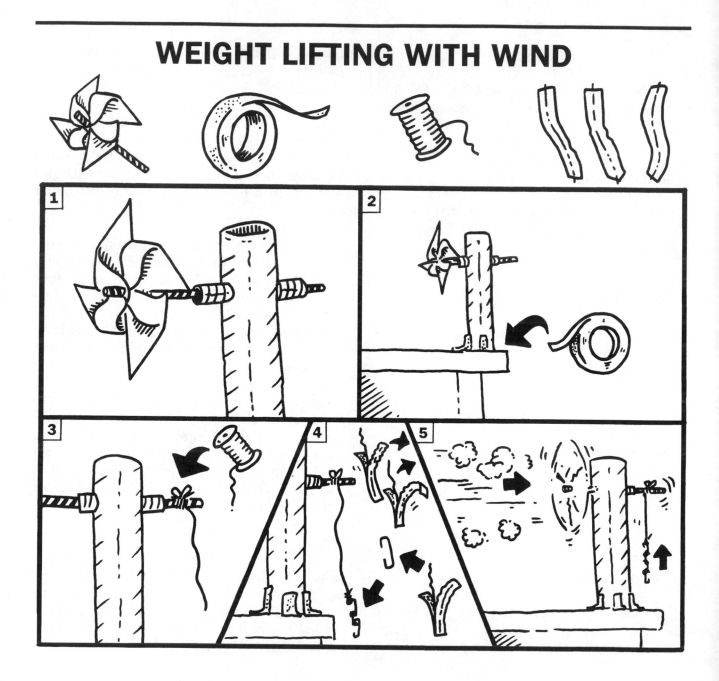

Materials

construction-paper pinwheel (previous activity)
masking tape
thread
metal twist ties

What to do

1 Make the pinwheel as directed.

2 Attach the paper-towel roll of the pinwheel to the corner of a table, using the masking tape to secure the roll. The blades of your pinwheel should face toward the table.

3 Securely attach a piece of thread to the back end of the windmill (the smaller straw should extend beyond the larger straw). Make sure the thread is hanging over the edge of the table.

4 Tear the paper off the twist ties, and bend the wires into the shape of a C. Attach the thread to one of the wire Cs. Then hook another C to the first one.

5 Blow on the windmill (or use a small fan or hair dryer), and watch it lift the Cs up. (Make sure the thread does not turn on the straw.) Add more Cs to the chain, and see how many the windmill can lift.

What happened

The way a windmill works is simple. The blades of the windmill catch the wind and are turned by it. The shafts that are attached to the blades also turn and generate energy to power other things. Wind-mills can be used to pump water or make electricity.

Did you know?

While windmills have been around for centuries, it wasn't until recently that the design for them has changed. Today's windmills have two or sometimes three blades, instead of the traditional four blades. These blades are lighter and spin faster. The faster the blades spin, the more energy they can create. One of the biggest windmills in the world is in Scotland. The propeller for this windmill is almost 150 feet (46 m) across. One of the world's greatest concentrations of windmills is in California, where there are fields filled with windfarms.

Wind is a renewable source of energy. Others include solar power, biomass (plant and animal wastes used for making fuel), and hydroelectric power (power from water).

EARTHWORM DAY

Making a worm composter is a fun way to actually see composting in action and to get some new pets at the same time. (NOTE: This experiment involves living creatures, so be kind and careful with them.)

Materials

large plastic tub with tight-fitting lid (or an old wooden box, barrel, or chest with a plastic bag or old carpet for a lid)

drill or hammer and nail

bedding such as shredded newspaper or cardboard, leaves, dried grass cuttings, dead plants, manure, or even peat moss

small amounts of sand and soil

shovel or stick

red worms, commonly called "red wigglers," or manure worms (available from bait stores or found in old barnyard manure piles)

food wastes, such as fruit and vegetable peelings, broken eggshells, coffee grounds, tea leaves, or breads

small container with lid

tray and bricks

What to do

The size of container you choose will depend on where you are going to store it and how much food wastes your family creates. A basic formula to follow is: 1 square foot (about 900 sq. cm) of surface area for each pound of household food wastes. Start with a large plastic container (or wooden box) about 24 inches (60 cm) long, 18 inches (45 cm) wide, and 12 inches (30 cm) high. This size will fit under most sinks or store easily on porches or balconies.

Once you have chosen your container, have an adult drill or poke holes every 2 inches (5 cm) along the top and bottom of each side of the container and 12 holes in the bottom. These holes in the container let air in and allow water to drain out. If you are using a plastic container, an adult will also have to drill holes in the lid.

1 Gather the bedding materials. Wet any dry material, so that it feels like a damp sponge. Add a handful of sand and one of soil to the bedding. Fill the container about three-fourths full.

2 Use the shovel or stick to lift and turn the bedding to stir it up and make some air pockets. This will help control odors and let the worms move freely.

3 Now add about 1 pound (454 g) of worms. Gently mix the worms into the bedding. Cover the container with the lid, or use an old carpet or plastic bag.

4 Keep the food scraps in a sealed container for 2 days before adding them to the compost mixture. (Do not use meat, bones, dairy products, or anything that has sugar or salt in it.)

5 When you add the scraps to feed your worms, make a hole in the bedding, dump the food scraps into this hole, and cover it up again. Use a different area of the compost each time you bury food scraps.

6 Place the bin anywhere it is warm, dark, and dry (under the sink, in the basement, or in a shady part of the balcony during warmer months of the year). Put the bin on bricks and place a tray under this to catch any excess water. (NOTE: Your worms will not run away or escape, because they would die of lack of food and moisture outside their comfortable home.)

7 After about two months of feeding your worms, there will be little bedding left. Now it's time to change the bedding and use your compost. Push the old bedding and the worms to one side of the container, and add new bedding to the other side of the container. Wait for one day; the worms will gradually move over to the new bedding. Take the old compost out, removing any worms and putting them back into the new bedding. Use the compost for planting soil and on your lawn and garden. WATCH OUT! If you see any small yellow cocoons, don't throw them out. They contain between 5 and 20 baby worms. Put them back into the new bedding.

Clean your worms' home every two months. Put a spider in the bin to eat any pesky fruit flies that might bother you.

What happened

At the front of the worm is its mouth, where the food goes in. The food then passes through the worm and is digested, or broken down, until it is passed out the other end as a waste material. The sand and soil provide grit that the worms use to help digest the food. These waste products look like tiny seeds and are called "casings." The organic worm casings can be removed after two to three months and mixed with your garden plants. Unlike a regular composting bin, your worm composter should not smell if it is properly working.

Did you know?

Your worms will grow to be about 3 inches (7.5 cm) long and will eat their own weight in garbage every 24 hours. The scraps will break down seven times faster than they would break down naturally in a dump. Composting is a natural way to turn organic waste into something useful for the environment. Worm composting is called *vermicomposting*. It increases soil fertility and processes organic waste. Worms are important because they put air into the soil, improve the soil quality, help the soil hold more water, and help create the best fertilizers in the world. Many fertilizers used today can contain toxic, or poisonous, ingredients. The fertilizers created by worms are all natural.

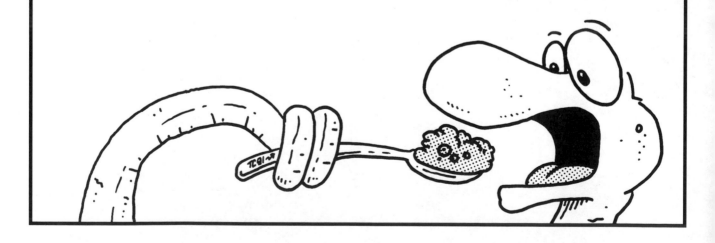

SCRATCH-AND-SNIFF PAPER

There's no mystery to making paper. How about your own scratch-and-sniff paper, made without destroying any trees?

Materials

about 100 pages of old newspaper, used paper from around the house, or light cardboard

blender or food processor

food coloring (optional)

dried mint, cinnamon, dried flowers, or other fragrances, such as almond or peppermint extract

cornstarch

old washtub, plastic wading pool, or big pan

2 pieces of nylon or wire screen (available at hardware stores) about 9 inches by 12 inches (22.5 cm by 30 cm)

spatula

rolling pin (optional)

What to do

Ask an adult for assistance in using the blender or processor.

1 Rip papers into small pieces about 1 inch by 1 inch (2.5 cm by 2.5 cm).

2 Put 1 cup (240 ml) of ripped paper into the blender, and add ¾ cup (180 ml) water. Add paper and water to the blender until it is about one-half full. Blend on low speed until the mixture forms a pulp. If necessary, add more water to make it move more easily.

3 For colored paper, add 10 drops of food coloring to this pulp and blend until mixed. Next add 3 drops of extract or 2 tablespoons (30 ml) of your chosen spice. For a shinier paper that is easier to write on, add 1 heaping tablespoon (25 ml) of cornstarch to the mixture. Blend all the ingredients together for about 30 seconds.

4 Place several layers of newspapers on the bottom of the washtub. Place one screen on top of this paper. Carefully pour the pulp mixture into the center of the screen. If the pulp is too thick, you may wish to add more water. Using a spatula, evenly distribute the pulp over the screen, leaving about 2 inches (5 cm) from the edge free.

5 Place the second screen over the pulp and cover with several layers of newspaper. Using a rolling pin or the palms of your hands, roll or push the excess water out of the pulp. Repeat this process several times, changing the newspaper as necessary to absorb more water, until most of the water is absorbed.

6 Lift the two layers of screen from the tub. Place the screen-covered pulp in a warm area on some newspaper and lay it flat to dry. Allow the paper to dry overnight. Once the paper is dry, trim it to any shape you like.

What happened

The waste paper was turned into a pulp. The pulp contains wood fibers because the newspaper was originally made from trees. These fibers stick together when the water is removed, leaving you with a piece of recycled paper. The fragrance of the paper will become stronger when you scratch it.

Did you know?

Paper can be recycled only three times, because the fibers get shorter and weaker each time the paper is recycled. Small amounts of new wood pulp can be added to recycled paper to make it stronger. Recycling paper is a good idea because 25 to 50 percent less energy is used to make recycled paper than to make new paper. This reduces the air pollution from newspaper making by 95 percent.

PORTABLE FRIDGE

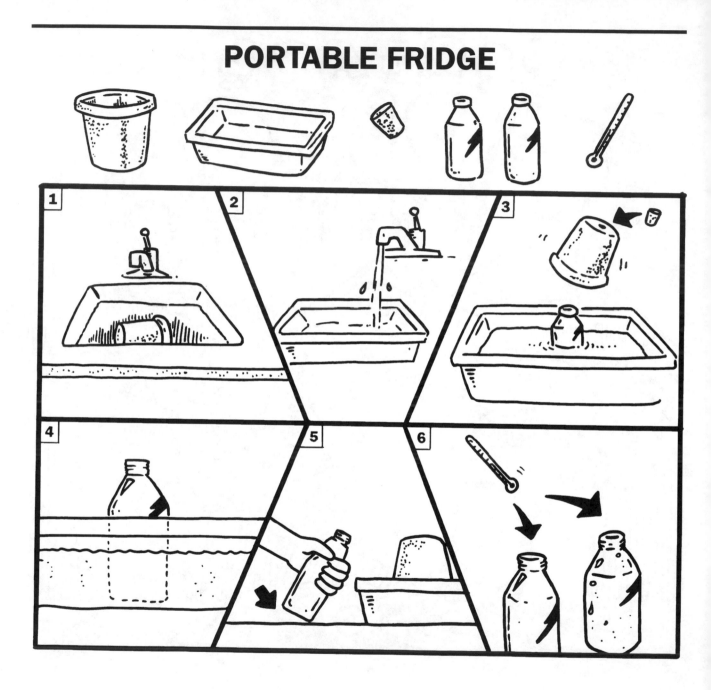

Refrigerators and air conditioners use CFCs (chlorofluorocarbons) for cooling. These CFCs are one of the main causes of the destruction of the ozone layer. Researchers are now working on ways to make refrigerators that don't use CFCs. In the meantime, here's a simple way to cool things without using any energy or CFCs.

Materials

clay flower pot or clay wine cooler

large pan

cork or something that will act as a stopper for the bottom of the flower pot, if there is a hole at the bottom of the pot

2 small cold bottles of juice

thermometer

What to do

1 Take the clay pot or cooler and soak it in cold water in a sink until it is wet all the way through (about 10 minutes).

2 Fill the pan about three-fourths full with cold tap water, and place it on a counter or table.

3 Stand an open bottle of juice in the water in the pan. (Make sure the top of the bottle is higher than the surface of the water.)

4 Turn the clay pot upside down over the bottle, plugging the hole (if any) with a cork stopper.

5 Place another open bottle of juice on the counter, next to the experiment.

6 Check the temperature of the 2 juices after 1 hour and then again after 2 hours. Which one is colder?

What happened

As the water evaporated from the clay pot, it took heat away from the air inside. That cooled the air under the pot so that the bottle stayed cool. The clay pot soaked up the water in the bowl. This water also evaporated, so the drink was kept cooler longer than the uncovered bottle.

Did you know?

CFCs were once thought to be a great invention: They are odorless, nontoxic, nonflammable, and noncorrosive (they don't make metals decay). CFCs are used to regulate temperatures in refrigerators and air conditioners, as well as in such places as zoos, hospitals, and office buildings. They are used to clean delicate electronic equipment and communication networks.

Despite the ban on CFCs in aerosols and other plastic products (like fast-food containers), getting rid of CFCs is a massive challenge. The best thing that you can do is to keep your refrigerator and air conditioner in good condition so the CFCs can't leak into the atmosphere.

WHY SHOULD MY WINDOW WEAR A COAT?

To *conserve* means "to save" or, put another way, "not to waste." This experiment will show you how insulation in your home conserves energy by keeping heat in (or in the summer, keeping cool air in).

Materials

pen and masking tape

5 small jars the same size, including lids

newspaper

elastic bands

old cotton T-shirt

thick towel and a washcloth

a box (larger than the jars)

boiling water

thermometer

What to do

1 Use the masking tape and pen to label each jar. Prepare the jars as follows: **a.** Wrap one jar with newspaper, using the elastic bands to keep the paper in place. Label this "Jar 1." **b.** Cut the sleeves off an old cotton T-shirt and put them aside. Wrap the rest of the T-shirt around the second jar, and secure with elastic bands. Label this "Jar 2." **c.** Tie a thick towel around the next jar. Label this "Jar 3." **d.** Label

a jar "Jar 4." Place it inside the box. Pack the space around the jar with crumpled newspaper. **e.** Leave one jar without anything around it. Label this "Jar 5."

2 Have an adult fill each jar to the top with boiling water. Then quickly screw the appropriate lid onto each jar. Cover each of the "insulated" jar's lids with the same type of material that you wrapped on the outside of the jar.

3 After one-half hour, record the room temperature. Then check the temperature of the water in each jar. Repeat this every half hour. Keep a record of the temperatures. See how long it took each of them to reach room temperature.

4 Try this experiment again, this time using ice water.

What happened

In the first experiment, the jars that kept the water the warmest were the ones with the best insulation. By creating a layer of air between the cold outside and the warm inside, the insulation helped stop the heat from escaping. The same principle also worked to keep the most insulated water cool for the longest time in the second experiment.

Did you know?

Whales have blubber and many animals have fur coats to keep them warm. Birds have a natural oil on their feathers to keep out the water. Some birds line their nests with paper for insulation, and rabbits line their burrows with moss for warmth. Nature's creatures are very smart, and we should follow their example. In addition to using commercial insulation, trees can help insulate homes. Trees and vines help shade your home in the summer and reduce cooling costs. In the winter, the trees lose their leaves and let the sun shine into your home, adding warmth while cutting down your heating cost.

TEA FOR TWO

If your parents don't put their used tea bags in a compost heap and just throw them out, stop—save a few. Here's a fun way to recycle them.

Materials

paper towels
bowl or dish
used tea bag
small flower or vegetable seeds
Note: Not all seeds will sprout, so, if you can, try this experiment with 2 or 3 tea bags with a seed, each in its own bowl.

What to do

1 Fold the paper towel into quarters, wet it completely, and place it in the middle of the bowl.

2 Flatten the tea bag and lay it in the center of the paper towel.

3 Cut a hole in the top of the tea bag. Then wet the tea bag.

4 Plant a seed in the wet tea bag.

5 Place the bowl in a sunny window. Add a little water to the tea bag each day.

6 When your seedling has grown enough (about 1 week to sprout and 3 to 4 weeks to grow), you may wish to replant it (tea bag and all) in the garden or in a pot with soil.

What happened

The tea bag provided the nutrients and the moisture that the seedling needed to grow.

Did you know?

Plants are amazing. Some plants can grow in salt water, some in sandy soils, and some in no soil at all. With the increase in pollution of our lands and water supplies, it may be necessary in the future to develop plants that adapt to harsher environments and are more resistant to pollutants.

Some different types of plants help each other by repelling insects and warding off diseases. Some good "buddies" include: garlic, which keeps many insects away from flowers and other plants; onions and chives, which prevent rust on carrots planted near them; mint, which keeps away butterflies that eat cabbage; and French marigolds, which are thought to help tomatoes and beans.

Give your plant a "buddy"!

CREATING ENVIRONMENTALLY FRIENDLY PRODUCTS

Next time you go shopping, observe how things are packaged. Which products are double wrapped or are in two or more boxes? Which products are in boxes that are much bigger than the product? What do you think happens to this extra packaging when you open the product? Do you think that this packaging is a waste? If this packaging isn't necessary, are the products that they contain necessary?

Some products you are buying may contain things that can harm both you and the environment, things that you don't really need. When you use a product every day, you naturally think it is safe, but sometimes this is not true. Products are sometimes recalled because it has been discovered that they may contain harmful ingredients. Even if a product is safe for you, it may still contain ingredients that harm the environment. Since the beginning of time, people have used natural products to clean themselves and their homes. You could check at your local natural foods store for many of them, but there are also many everyday products you can make cheaply and safely at home. This section contains some simple experiments and activities for making your own natural products.

RAISING MONEY FOR THE ENVIRONMENT

Before you go on to the experiments, ask yourself this: Can I help save the environment and help environmental groups at the same time? The answer is YES. In order to operate, most environmental groups need volunteers and money. Volunteering is a wonderful idea, but it takes a lot of time and effort. If you feel you can't help out that much because you have too much schoolwork and you don't have money to give these groups, you can still help. Organize a sale at your school. You and your friends can make environmentally friendly products and sell them at the sale. You can also have a used toy sale and use the money for these groups. Have a recycling project started at school and use any money raised for other environmental causes. There are many organizations that need your help. We have listed a sampling of these groups in the back of the book. You can check your local telephone directory for other environmental organizations in your area. Before you donate money to any group, have an adult find out what the group will be doing with the money. Choose an organization you feel will be putting your money to good use.

NO EXCUSES SOAP

The soap you buy in stores is not required by law to list its ingredients. Most soaps are made from a combination of animal and vegetable fats. But soap can contain substances that can harm both you and the environment. What could be better than washing yourself with environmentally safe soap you have made yourself?

Materials

soap flakes

microwavable bowl or old pot for cooking

glycerine (available at drugstores)

rubbing alcohol

cinnamon or paprika (optional)

food coloring

old muffin tins, old molds, or small plastic containers

What to do

1 Put 1 cup (240 ml) of soap flakes in a microwavable bowl.

2 Add ⅓ cup (80 ml) of glycerine and 2 tablespoons (30 ml) of rubbing alcohol to the soap flakes and stir. Gently add ⅛ cup (30 ml) of water to the mixture and stir. (NOTE: You can vary the amounts of glycerine and rubbing alcohol to make the soap more opaque or softer.)

3 If you want a rust-colored soap that smells like cinnamon, you can add about 1 tablespoon (15 ml) of cinnamon to the mixture. If you want a spicy soap that has a coral color, add 1 tablespoon (15 ml) of paprika. If you'd like just a colored soap, you can add a drop of natural food coloring.

Have an adult help you with the next steps.

4 Microwave the soap mixture until it comes to a boil. If you do not have a microwave oven, put the mixture in a pot on the stove over low heat and slowly bring to a boil.

5 As soon as the mixture has boiled, put it in a safe place to cool. Stir the mixture occasionally while it is cooling.

6 When the mixture is cool and clear but still liquid, pour it into molds and allow to set until firm. This may take several hours.

7 Turn the molds upside down and take out the soaps. If the soap sticks, run a knife around the edge of the mold and pry the soap out. If you wish, you may wrap the soaps in tissue paper until you are ready to use them.

What happened

In this experiment, the glycerine (which is an oil) combined with the soap flakes (which are alkaline, or not acidic) to produce the soap. This is a very mild and non-irritating soap because it contains no lyes (which are harsh and dry your skin) and contains only natural ingredients.

Did you know?

Before television, VCRs, and video games, people used to get together and make soaps, candles, and preserves. Townspeople would gather and make enough of these items to last for a season. Sharing the work was not only the best way of making large amounts of soap, but it was a great form of entertainment. Think how much fun it would be to have a soap-making event at your school or even a soap-making birthday party.

BUBBLE BONANZA

BUBBLE BATH

Each year there are complaints about irritations, rashes, and infections that people may have gotten from bath products. This is especially true for children, who have the most sensitive skin. Some bath products contain detergents, ethanol (a form of alcohol), and colorings, which may be harmful to people. You may not be crazy about taking baths, but how about a nice bubble bath with bubble bath liquid that you made yourself?

Materials

empty 2 quart (2 l) bottle or container

1 quart (960 ml) water

1 cup (240 ml) liquid castile soap (available from health-food stores)

3 fluid ounces (90 ml) glycerine (from drugstores)

4 drops perfume or a natural fragrance

funnel   bottles with tops

What to do

1 Mix the water, soap, and glycerine together in the large, empty bottle or container. Blend them well.

2 Add perfume 1 drop at a time until it smells the way you like it. (It won't smell as strong when put in the bathwater.)

3 Place the funnel in the top of one of the bottles. Carefully pour the bath liquid into the bottle. Continue with each bottle until you have used up all the bath liquid.

What happened

You made a fun, inexpensive product that won't harm the environment.

BUBBLE SOLUTION TO A BORING DAY

It's a great day outside, but you haven't got any bubble solution to blow bubbles with. But wait—here's a recipe to save the day.

Materials

¼ cup (60 ml) glycerine
½ cup (120 ml) dishwashing liquid
1 cup (240 ml) warm water
¼ cup (60 ml) light corn syrup
1 quart (960 ml) mayonnaise jar
long-handled spoon or stirrer

What to do

1 Pour glycerine, dishwashing liquid, water, and corn syrup into the jar.

2 Stir gently until blended.

3 Dip any bubble blower into the solution and have fun blowing bubbles!

NOTE: You can vary the amount of glycerine for different types of solution.

BUBBLE BLOWER

Materials

plastic soft-drink bottle   felt marker
sharp knife   scissors

What to do

Ask an adult to help you make the bubble blower.

1 Using a felt marker, draw a line around the bottle on an angle as shown.

2 Ask your adult to use the knife to cut an opening large enough for the tip of the scissors to fit into.

3 Following the line, cut the bottle in two. Dip the cut end of the bottle into the solution and use it as a bubble blower by blowing through the neck of the bottle.

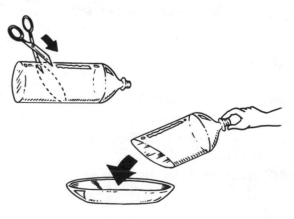

MAKE FLEAS FLEE

If you own a cat or a dog, you probably have experienced the "joy" of fleas. Many flea collars, powders, and sprays are harmful not only to the fleas, but also to you and your pets. Next time you are in a store, read the warning label on a flea product. It's enough to scare both you and the fleas away! Here are some homemade solutions to the flea problem—solutions that are safe and inexpensive.

Materials

bowl	water
lavender-oil extract	saucepan
rock salt	
skin of an orange	
blender	

What to do

SOLUTION 1

1 In a bowl, add about 2 ounces (60 ml) of lavender oil to 3 quarts (2.85 l) of rock salt. Toss lightly until oil is absorbed.

2 Place several tablespoons (1 tablespoon=15 ml) of this mixture under sofas, rugs, bedroom furniture, and other things that don't get moved that often.

3 If you can't find lavender oil, you can sprinkle small amounts of diatomaceous earth (available at hardware stores) on your carpets and floors and around baseboards. This will have the same effect on the fleas as the lavender oil and rock salt.

SOLUTION 2

1 Have an adult process the skin of an orange in a blender or food processor.

2 Add about 1 cup (240 ml) of water to the orange skin and blend.

3 Pour the mixture into a small saucepan. Heat on a stove until it boils. Lower the heat and cook for **5** minutes.

4 When the pulp has cooled, smooth some of the liquid onto your pet's fur.

What happened

We think that certain smells, like lavender and orange, are nice, but fleas hate these smells. It drives them crazy and they leave. To get rid of fleas or to kill them without using chemicals, all you have to do is keep things clean and repel the fleas with odors they can't stand.

Did you know?

Adult fleas live off the blood of animals and are very hard to kill. They have hard bodies that make them difficult to "squish." Fleas can jump distances of up to 3 feet. A female flea can lay between 20 and 30 eggs in one day and can continue laying this many eggs for 6 to 9 months. This means that a single female flea can produce up to 8,000 eggs in 9 months. If left alone, each of the flea's eggs will hatch in about 3 weeks. If half of these fleas are females and start laying eggs, this will result in about 500 eggs per day being laid, or 15,000 eggs per month!

MOTHS ARE EATING MY CLOTHES

If you've ever been near mothballs, you know how terrible they smell. Commercial mothballs carry warning labels that tell you that the product is harmful if swallowed and that you should not touch them or breathe their vapor. This is silly, if you think about it. How can you use the mothballs without smelling them? You can make your own safe and environmentally friendly mothballs that also are great gifts.

Materials

small bowl	sweet marjoram
crushed cinnamon	lavender
thyme	mint
rosemary	small squares of cloth
sage	ribbon

What to do

1 Mix the herbs and spices together in a bowl.

2 Place several tablespoons of this mixture in the middle of a square of cloth.

3 Bring the corners of the cloth together, and tie with a ribbon. You have made a sachet (sa-shay).

4 Place these sachets in drawers and closets. Replace every 3 or 4 months.

What happened

As with fleas, moths are attracted to certain smells and repelled by others. The mixture you made may smell great to you, but it grosses out moths.

HAIR'S LOOKING AT YOU, KID

Some shampoos may contain harmful ingredients such as ammonia, coloring, ethanol, formaldehyde, nitrates, and even plastics (PVP). If you buy shampoo, make sure to read the labels or choose one with all natural ingredients. Here's a shampoo that's safe for you and the environment!

Materials

1 cup (240 ml) pure liquid castile soap (available from health-food stores)
¼ cup (60 ml) olive oil
2 cups (480 ml) distilled water
egg
2 to 3 drops almond or mint extract (if desired)

blender
old bottles

What to do

1 Have an adult place the castile soap, olive oil, water, and egg in a blender. Mix on high for about 10 seconds.

2 Carefully pour your shampoo into the bottles. Store the shampoo in the refrigerator when you are not using it. After two weeks, the shampoo goes bad; you should then put it in your compost heap to help the soil. If you want a shampoo that lasts longer, don't use the egg in your shampoo.

SAVE A TREE

Much of the garbage that is thrown away could be reused or recycled. Instead of throwing away the newspaper each day, here's one way you can make a useful product from it.

Materials

old newspapers
cedar or other wood chips, or crushed pine cones
twine or string
old plastic wading pool or large washtub
water
salt

What to do

1 Find a nice, dry place on a lawn or patio to work on. Place about 20 to 30 large sheets of newspaper together.

2 Add about 1 cup (240 ml) of shavings or crushed pine cones between about every 8 pages.

3 Tightly roll each section and tie loosely at each end (but not so loose that the string falls off).

4 Fill the pool with water and enough chips, pine cones, or other nice-smelling woods to cover about half of the water's surface. Add about 3 cups (720 ml) of salt to the water (this will make the logs burn red).

5 Place your logs in the water, turning them several times to cover with water. Leave the logs in the pool for 1 week, remembering to turn them at least once per day.

6 When the week is up, remove the logs and place them in a safe area to dry. When your logs have dried completely, they are ready to burn. (Be sure to use them safely, just like real logs, with adult supervision.)

What happened

You have just saved a tree and made a recycled product. During the soaking process, the roll absorbed the water solution, which will make it burn longer after it has dried out.

Did you know?

Every day there are about 72 million newspapers sold in the United States and Canada. And over 70 percent of these papers are just thrown away. This means that about 80,000 trees are thrown into dumps each day. Paper and paperboard make up almost one-third of all landfill wastes. By recycling paper, we not only save trees but also reduce pollution and landfills.

ENVIRONMENTAL ORGANIZATIONS

Listed here are some of the many environmental organizations that are working to save our planet. If you want more information or want to find out what you can do to help, call or write them. They are always more than happy to speak with you.

UNITED STATES

Acid Rain Foundation
1630 Blackhawk Hills
St. Paul, MN 55122
(612) 455-7719

American Forestry Association
1516 P Street NW
Washington, DC 20005
(202) 667-3300

Americans for the Environment
1400 16th Street NW
Washington, DC 20036
(202) 547-8000

CARE for the Earth
PO Box 289
Sacramento, CA 94101
(415) 781-1585

Citizens for a Better Environment
942 Market Street #505
San Francisco, CA 94102
(415) 788-0690

Coalition for Recyclable Wastes
1525 New Hampshire Avenue
    NW
Washington, DC 20036
(202) 842-3526

EarthSave Foundation
PO Box 949
Felton, CA 05018-0949
(408) 423-4069

Environmental Action
1525 New Hampshire Avenue
    NW
Washington, DC 20036
(202) 745-4870

Environmental Defense Fund
257 Park Avenue South
New York, NY 10010
(212) 505-2100

Friends of the Earth
530 7th Street SE
Washington, DC 20003
(202) 543-4312

Greenpeace
PO Box 3720
Washington, DC 20007
(202) 462-1177

International Wildlife Coalition
1807 H Street NW
Washington, DC 20006
(202) 347-0822

National Audubon Society
950 Third Avenue
New York, NY 10022
(212) 832-3200

National Wildlife Federation
1412 16th Street NW
Washington, DC 20036-2266
(202) 797-6800

Project Earth
PO Box 1031
Evergreen, CO 80439
(303) 647-0271

Sierra Club
730 Polk Street
San Francisco, CA 94109
(415) 776-2211

U.S. Environmental Protection
    Agency
401 M Street SW
Washington, DC 20460
(202) 382-4627

The Wilderness Society
1400 I Street
Washington, DC 20005
(202) 842-3400

Worldwatch Institute
1776 Massachusetts Avenue
    NW
Washington, DC 20036
(202) 452-1999

CANADA

Alberta Environment Network
10511 Saskatchewan Drive
Edmonton, Alberta T6E 4S1
(403) 433-9302

B.C. Environmental Network
2150 Maple Street
Vancouver, BC V6J 3T3
(604) 733-2400

Canadian Coalition on Acid Rain
112 St.Clair Avenue West
Toronto, Ontario M4V 2Y3
(416) 968-2135

Canadian Nature Federation
453 Sussex Drive
Ottawa, Ontario K1N 6Z4
(613) 238-6154

Canadian Wildlife Federation
1673 Carling Avenue
Ottawa, Ontario K2A 3Z1
(613) 725-2191

Ecology Action Centre
#520 - 1657 Barrington Street
Halifax, Nova Scotia B3J 2A1
(902) 454-7828

Friends of the Earth
251 Laurier Avenue West
Ottawa, Ontario K1P 5J6
(613) 230-3352

Greenpeace
578 Bloor Street West
Toronto, Ontario M5G 1K1
(416) 538-6470

Manitoba Environmental Network
PO Box 3125
Winnipeg, Manitoba R3C 4E6
(204) 956-1468

Ontario Environmental Network
PO Box 125, Station P
Toronto, Ontario M5S 2S7
(416) 925-1322

Rainforest Action Society
PO Box 46695 Station G
Vancouver, BC V6R 4K8
(604) 734-8772

Saskatchewan Eco-Network
205-219 22nd Street East
Saskatoon, Saskatchewan
   S7K 0G4
(306) 665-1915

Sierra Club of Ontario
2316 Queens Street East
Toronto, Ontario M4E 1G8
(416) 698-8446

Sierra Club of Western Canada
620 View Street #314
Victoria, BC V8W 3T8
(604) 386-5255

Western Canada Wilderness
   Committee
20 Water Street
Vancouver, BC V6B 1A4
(604) 683-8220

World Wildlife Fund Canada
50 St. Clair Avenue East
Toronto, Ontario M5T 1N8
(416) 923-8173

UNITED KINGDOM

Conservation Society
12A Guilford Street
Chertsey, Surrey, England

Earth First (England)
57 Wood Lane
Greasby, Wirral L49 ZPU,
   England

Earth First (Scotland)
6 Mansfield Place
Edinburgh EH3 6LE, Scotland

Earthwatch Europe
29 Coniston Avenue
Headington, Oxford OX3 OAN,
   England

Friends of the Earth
Harbour View, Entry
County Cork, Ireland

Friends of the Earth
26-28 Underwood Street
London N1 75Q, England
(01) 490-1555

World Forest Campaign
6 Glebe Street
Oxford OX4 1DG, England

World Wildlife Fund
Panda House
11 Ockford Road
Goldaming, Surrey, England

INDEX